FOR THE DARK

WILLIAM COLLINS WATTERSON

Mellen Poetry Press

Library of Congress Cataloging-in-Publication Data

Watterson, William Collins.
  For the dark / William Collins Watterson.
    p. cm.
  ISBN 0-7734-0006-0
  I. Title.
  PS3573.A864F67   1992
  811'.54--dc20   92-20756
                                                                        CIP

Mellen Poetry Press
The Edwin Mellen Press
Box 450
Lewiston, New York 14092

Printed in the United States of America

For Rosalie Colie, if she were here . . .

Finish, good lady, the bright day is done,
And we are for the dark . . .

Antony and Cleopatra

CONTENTS

"The Humanist" first appeared in *The Chronicle of Higher Education*, "October" in *Axis*, "Monhegan Revisited" in *Habitat*, "Teaching My Son to Talk," "On Reading Cavafy," and "Thinking of Jackson Pollock" in *The Kenyon Review*, "Nightscape with Doves" in *The New Yorker*, "April" in the *Maine Sunday Telegram*, "To a Young Museum Guard" and "Eine Kleine Nachtmusik" in *Poetry*, "Walt Whitman, Night Nurse," "Evensong at Christ Church," "Drying Out," "Elegy for Papa," and "Summer Saturday" in the *Warren Wilson Review*, "The Iconoclast," "Imagination MGM Style," "Flagstad Remembers" in *Studia Mystica*, "Beatus Ille" in *The Sewanee Review*.

POINT BLANK

Hold still and smile.
You never feel a thing
at point blank range
except the numbing—
who would call that strange?

Can't you see it? Don't you know?
You pose a dozen times a day
for skilled photographers
who've learned to have their way
with you, focusing and clicking,
then sticking you without delay
in albums of forgotten light.

Take hear. Don't flinch,
and never mind the pain.
The killing camera doesn't lie:
You'll never be the man you were again.

GUSSIE

Everybody knew Gussie:
the stout posture of chest
ample as Brünhilde's
even at seventy,
the strong straight arms
that lugged the shopping bags
with fifteen pounds of canned cat food
apiece,
the symmetry of her gait
as she marched down the same old streets,
winter and summer,
come snow or high humidity
to supermarkets and back again
to that decaying house of her father,
its single Victorian tower
like a battlement or a church
pawing its way toward heaven.

For forty years she salvaged:
tortoise shells, calicos, and Russian blues,
orange tigers and grey
Siamese, Persians, and Angoras,
mothers with their young, Toms,
orphans of both sexes (fixed and unfixed),
the one-eyed, the tailless, and the lame,
money cats all who ate away
the last of an old immigrant's fortune,
her father's horsehair sofas in the parlor

2

year-round creches of kittens,
the bookcases living libraries
and bowls of brown chow
served like cocktail snacks
on sideboards scratched to shreds.

Gussie knew nobody but waved to all
briskly, winter and summer,
too busy on her errands to stop,
her kindness like a clock
Teutonic and precise
with hands always on time
though behind the impassive face
neighbors said the tooth of a gear was gone
her escapement imperfect
like the gap in an alley fighter's grin.

The postman found her in January
frozen on the floor.
On her breast a mackerel tabby purred:
his motor ran twenty-four hours
after the corpse was cold.

ORPHAN: SAIGON 1970

Twenty-dollar boom-boom and here I am,
another yellow bastard, twelve years old,
a mite embarrassing to Uncle Sam,
who bought the farm, then left me in the cold.
A chopper got my mother on the run;
its grassed-up gunner, giddy, popped away
until he dropped her in the paddied sun,
heart burst clean from a blond soldier's spray.
Who saved my ass? Some priest, a holy man,
one lucky Father for a boy to know;
He tries to listen but he's quick to tan,
his hand hot napalm where the red don't show.
     Find a way to Frisco. Drink Coke all day.
     I'm going to make some Yankees pay and pay.

THE HUMANIST

All day he sits at a desk
churning out footnotes
which are the poetry left his life,
the last word on history.

His posture aches
and he knows the pain of not being able
to give his work away,
the pathos of self-addressed stamped envelopes,
but always he must stand faster,
the fruits of his toil
cast before deans and editors
as of no worth,
his labor the lilies
of some field.
He sings to empty houses.

Science at least
might have served his self-importance
better.
He could have published negative results,
made something of nothing,
amounted to more.

As it is, he thinks only
of the past,
of the idea he had that devotion
was once the measure of all things.

FRESHMAN, HARVARD YARD

His eyes unbearably blue
like a fjord too cold
to swim in.
Old polo shirt
green as a meadow
and khakis that cleave
as he goes walking,
his athlete's thigh
drummed absent-mindedly by Vergil,
the eclogues stiff as a board
but virginal
in spanking Oxford wrappers
of prep-school pink.
Smart as a rattan
the Mantuan's art,
though the text itself holds still,
the pain of words like waves
whipped halcyon by storm.

In the trees the dons lurk,
mumbling platonists
who would know without desiring
but cannot,
so many Corydons
for whom the arc and slope
of flesh remembered
flexes to pure form.
It is when the body fades

and boys grow younger
that the soul is born,
a far-off vessel
glinting like gold dust
on undulating curves of the sea.
Beauty must be calm, they say,
like the form of his perfectly thoughtless arm,
now rising, now falling.

A MEMORY OF JAMES WRIGHT

In Ohio on a jag
he intoned at Oberlin:
"Who put the overalls in Mrs. Murphy's chowder?"
At greener English Kenyon
he contained himself,
began with "Winter Remembered" got by heart
and said the piece for Ransom,
the gentleman trying hard to hear,
his head inclined to Lowell perhaps
in the icy echoes of Ascension Hall.

In the poems between poems
he cursed Kent State,
the bull muscles of his neck
knotted and angry,
the wine-dark kindness of his eyes
like Indian Summer.

Where courteous Dekes tapped kegs
the white head bowed again,
his half-glass golden as the day failed:
"These days suicides get high grades
for feeling, but a poet will find God
in darkness and in light,
in hunger and satiety."
Comely the nightfall under roots and stars,
but we go soon enough
beneath the sobering shales.

Later, his master out of earshot
like a shade, Wright muttered:
"Roethke didn't drown by accident,
you know.
He swam himself to death
in the cruel blue lanes of a college pool."

Outside in the twilight it was Springtime.
Nighthawk and thrush, phoebe and shrike,
made tumult with the tongues of many birds.

SEMINAR

They watch me like a t.v. turned down low
and now I am watching them watch me,
their faces blank as endpapers
in books they will never read.

I am, apparently, a rerun,
just words but no music,
my "teacher knows best" voice a drag
no matter how much I modulate,
a one-man show less commercial interruptions,
my rating lower than I know.

When the hour ends I unplug myself,
my cord a prehensile tail
that slithers like a whip.

When the screen goes dark
the Keats ode fails
like perfect flora frozen in the shale.

EVENSONG AT CHRIST CHURCH

After two world wars and the death of God,
small Saxons bawl their pater nosters still
like ranks of putti, spanked,who kiss the rod,
round lips phonetic of the Father's will.
This nave is empty, only tourists hear
the vaulting din of English discipline,
its harped hosannas weary form the years
of weeping bitters in a stiff pink gin.
Past pride, past lust, post twilight empire now
the word once flesh is but a single flash
of holy dove, a lambent afterglow
alight in one rose window like a gash.
    Blond hair. Blue eyes. Boys penitently late.
    Red pickled cherries on a snow-white plate.

MIDDLE SCHOOL

The diamond emerald-green
where a stand of bone-white birches
twigs an endless curve of sky.
Young athletes old sinners now,
the sinews in their arms
sagging like bookstraps
from the strain.

You played at outfield here
but went shallow,
the coach who saved you
and saved you
cradled these twenty years
in the all-mothering earth.

From booze to broads
then back again,
the usual bad business
as he swung and missed
and swung again
at the straight hard pitches
of your youth.

Though you have known strike
after strike after strike
here you bat at knuckled memories
like the Sun.

CROSSING BROOKLYN BRIDGE

Behind me Carroll Gardens where my friend Gennaro
lives.
I can still see his cheeky brothers,
plump-faced putti with ripe olive eyes,
still hear high shrieks of delight
as they grin at strangers from the doorway
then run inside to hide.
On the sidewalk their grandfather, pure Sicilian,
sits in his green-plaid plastic lawn chair like a throne,
spits as the mood takes him any which way into wind,
the same wind perhaps that blew him to this
(from Messina, 1906, to steerage then a seat of honor
on the street) though maybe another.
Tomato and basil linger on the air,
their sweet simmer a *sine qua non* of summer.
A pregnant sister smiles as I pass,
looks up from the family of marigolds
she has been tending in a windowbox.

I am bound for SoHo and another gallery opening,
the state of art an upscale warehouse

where canvasses all concept and no craft
will stare me down,
the painter's Montrachet in jelly glasses
a priceless joke that only rich Bohemians
can afford.
Pale faces tight as lampshades
will shed hushed light
on bold aesthetic motives, on passion, on AIDS,
on the City's science of living and dying
on the edge.

To reach Manhattan
I will brave this bridge at a great height,
the blue of harbor and sky
a reciprocity as in Boudin
where heaven mirrors water,
where when you fall — up or down —
it will be through river light
that lands you lucky on your feet
with a gypsy cab to carry you
the rest of the way.

No seconds now for Berryman or Crane,
for mistakes made metaphors
for that bridge to the unwordable
cabled like a lyre
and stretching the whole arch span of it.
Today foot traffic keeps me on the verge —
cordovans, earth shoes, sandals, jogging pumps,

men and women like Mercury with wings at heels,
their faces on fire with life like Whitman's strangers
whose bright electric eyes give me that look that says
somewhere they will be waiting for me.

For their sake, for the sake of who's ahead
or might be next I keep on moving,
the human flow I go with now, alive,
never to be repeated, never satisfied.
I whistle. I quicken my step.
I salute the white gull for a moment poised
and motionless on the downdraft.

Love, love that has brought me to this
will find a way to lift me back.

TEACHING SUMMER SCHOOL
(Maine, 1983)

Children of the pure clear word,
the woods will darken soon
as in the glade of Actaeon
tenebrous and frenzied
where virgins dallied till the day was gone.

Remember the deer your fathers' dogs dragged down?
The truth of love unlooked for comes like that.
Upside down and dangling,
your glazed eyes sway in shadows.

Comes a time you'll know you're there.
A twig will snap, the bay of hounds
reverberate where silence chills
the pond to glass.

You are lonely. You are running.
They are gaining in fresh snow
slashed with sumac.
At bay and baffled,
not comprehending how,
nothing you know can save you.

VAN GOGH'S SUNFLOWERS

To hold those haggard faces in my hands,
radiant and punished in the frost light,

as if such giants might be windmills,
their blades churning like petals

as brown eyes battered blind
behold their executioners,

the crows sharp-beaked as furies
repeating their assault.

The search for seeds is endless,
but they can never find their fill.

A solitary bird, swart blue with silken wing
struts in the foreground

his famine a vain black maw
and yet I hardly notice him

here in this October
where flowers burn up heaven, earth

the imperial sun itself
with life, with light, with yellow

deafening all my senses
in a final blaze of field.

The black bird, no less than I,
is casual, inconsequential.

SALON DES REFUSÉS

I hired the hall myself
and sat there for years
amid the failed perspectives
and muddy pigments,
the landscape of my life
a glade Corot passed over
on the golden road to Arcady.
Nobody came.

To have missed the moment of art
and not know why —
to not have seen
the lilies of Monet on fire
for everyone but me —
and yet this filling up of space
with shape and color
fears the dark
more surely than the stretcher's
blinding white.

My stains have staunched the blankness.

"Ché gelida manina?"

The day I put my brush down
is the day I die.

ON A LATE LANDSCAPE BY GEORGE INNESS
(For Ann Lofquist)

Coppery sky. Dark trees.
Before the heavens break
a menace of far thunder,
the billows' edge burnished
like an old penny lost
through the crack
of a farmhouse floor.

In a pasture to the left
an old Holstein kneels
in shadow,
the black of her coat
devouring what's left of the white
in the ruminating twilight.

It is Montclair, 1893.
He is going to die soon.
At the vanishing point
where he lingers
in a trick too true of perspective
a single red maple shines.
He has caught it in the secret shimmer
of storms,
in that halo not of this earth
which says the gods have given us eyes.

Though the first cold drops may fall
any second now
he does not hurry
the studied sure brushwork
that is his only ease.

If the rainbow comes, he will paint it.

THINKING OF JACKSON POLLOCK

*When I am in my painting, I'm not aware of what
I'm doing. It is only after a sort of "get
acquainted" period that I see what I have been
about. I have no fears about making changes,
destroying the image, etc., because the
painting has a life of its own.*

J.P. 1947

The woods are a complicated thicket of lines
parallel and skewed aand intersecting
where deep inside huge shapes
move in shadow
and I once heard a shot ring out
echoing as if in anger through winter air.
A patch of something stained the snow
(rusty pine needles or maybe blood)
and a woodpecker climbed a tree upside down.
It is not a question of who died there
but of who is dying this very moment
where the certainty of sight fails.

I will wait a child forever at the edge
of these dark woods
trying to make sense of a cry
half animal, half human
where the shape of a strange body fell
lifeless in the snow.
Should I enter the tangle at last

(but I won't because it's twilight
and I know that I'm afraid),
I would see that I am part of the complication,
a dark shape myself
murdered by the thought of an invisible other
where a bullet still rings
and a crested bird with black and white wings
lined like a thicket
hops on a fretted bole.
He is dancing the delight of my unknowing.

SUMMER SATURDAY

It is a hot July afternoon
and I am watching the boy across the street
mow the family lawn.
I can see him but he can't see me.
He is wearing red and yellow surfing jambs
of Hawaiian implications —
nothing else —
and going at things more or less
with a vengeance,
the way teenagers do.
His chiselled curls
droop with blond exertion,
and the curve of his thigh
reminds me of a youthful David
by Donatello,
the Walkman at his hip
swaying like a sling.
He is thinking that tonight he will take
his girl friend out in his father's car,
that they will drive around for awhile
and maybe drink a little
and that if all goes well
he will take her in the dew
of early morning.
The hum of his motor oppresses me,
so I turn away from the window
and head for the icebox

ivory-smooth as a coffin.
There's nothing like a cold beer,
I think, after the grass is cut
on a hot July afternoon.

ON READING CAVAFY

Without hope, in love with the history
that doomed you,
you hung on for centuries
in a city of rosewater and brine,
mud and myrhh, this Alexandria
whore of all desire
and pitiless as the Farshooter's glint
on distant waves
or the wider ocean of an ephebe's eyes.
Through the tavern haze of years
I see you drowning in your dream,
in depths cloudless as unmixed ouzo,
in the small oblivion of a stranger's smile.

How well your nostrils knew it,
the odor of decay nearest the root
where Ptolemies in the earth
mulched the stiff papyrus.
Your stylus mastered the emptiness
of paper,
but the hollow of your groin was hapless,
the boys there pale as muskrose
in Elysian darkness.

Once you saw a working-class Adonis
shed his cinnamon-colored suit on the beach
then stride with adolescent calm
into the repeating waves.

Your feathered talons
longed for that stark thigh,
and twenty years later you wrote a poem
about the moment, unconsummated,
your tongue on fire
and Clio your only audience.
Those wide eyes ripe as olives —
were they Attic or Egyptian?
Even you could not remember.

Mnemosyne nursed you
but in her womb there is only the one idea,
the idea of academic Plato
with his heaven for all the flesh
lost but perfect forever
as if the salt of memory
could cure past stench
the flyblown forms of time.

On the strand a boy's delicate footprints
run into the sea:
It is as if his golden ankles
had suddenly sprouted wings.

ELEGY FOR PAPA (1899-1961)

Where the thicket clears
a man in a red jacket waits
for the old buck
rushing after rut for freedom
and the open spaces.

A bullet stops the brain
then bladeflash carves the haunch.
Upside down and helpless —
horned head limp —
his glazed eyes sway in shadows.

In July wheat sheen gilds a field
where an old man sits
shotgun poised between his knees
(impasto of first blood
like a brash red brushstroke by Corot).
Clarity swims in the blue eyes,
clarity of twilight
where black duennas pray
that day might die
indifferent as a matador,
sober and slim in the gored afternoon.

Remember the way he wrote
the arc and dip of a hooked rainbow,
silver bull rippling in sunlight
as if his heart would burst,
then diving down forever into night?

Now paint his silence with you words.

JOHN BERRYMAN

In the end he knew he could fly,
booze and the quill pricks
of heroin
having numbed the body's knowledge
of itself,
high-strung and restless
on the edge.

Mistakes made metaphors —
his bridge to the unwordable
cabled like a lyre
that stretched the whole arch span of it —
did he veer
in the fluted downdrafts
of his rushing,
his dream a dip of swallows
as in Keats,
rising and falling,
rising and falling,
twittering to himself
the dark music?

Icarus. Orpheus. Man bird.
Impatient for Parnassus,
he banked on the blankness
of heaven
and penned no note for earthbounds,
plume poised in midair
for the plunge.

28

IMAGINATION MGM STYLE

The Romantics made you their Frankenstein,
a grotesquerie of parts
botched from poetry, philosophy,
the Gothic caverns of a twilit faith
snatched from the vault
and charged with new life.

The result?
A monster to haunt science,
gigantic but a little bumbling
and yes, a bit of an automaton,
terrorizing the town
and decimating peasants,
though strangely tender to the little girl.

Derrida burned you out
(the common sense of crowds?
more likely the baron in disguise),
the light he held against your private parts
revealing the perfect nothingness,
that fire you were born to fear
renouncing the oxygen it ate.

What's left is text,
each piece assigned
its rightful box again,
not body but the charred remains,
awaiting the next mad humanist.

NAMING THE WHITE CHAOS LOVE

Though never quite together
there is nothing not in this poem
of yours and mine,
in the space between letters,
in the small breaths between words,
in the larger breaths
at the end of some lines,
in the emptiness of margins
where the mind pauses
and without which
the poem would not be possible.

I name the white chaos love
(spilling the black blood
of arrogant paroles)
and say that on that silence
everything depends,
the poem itself depends
its enslavement to the world complete.

Though I weave a text
secure enough and fine
and everything between us
passes through it
this way and that

without your chaos
I cannot keep the whiteness there.

DRYING OUT
New Orleans, 1988

The road winds down but not quite out,
so familiar and circuitous
it must lead home.
The levees cannot last, they say,
though the sun at least
seems sure of himself,
his solstice a foundry
prodigal and golden
in winter's solitary transit.

In Audubon Park the white tiger
stalks invisible prey,
her nervous circles
pure as habit.

Where the river runs wider, colder,
its Christmas tinsel sheen a travesty,
new currents underneath the mirror
shift and shift

and now you must be deft enough
to pick your way across —
holding your breath on tiptoe —
the glass below you brittle and a-churn,
one impossible step at a time.

EINE KLEINE NACHTMUSIK

"Music to hear. Why hear'st thou music sadly?"

For Richard L. Chittim

A Bach partita builds its mansion in the air.
The cellist, metaphysical, severe,
summons into sound abstraction after abstraction,
his concentration so complete that when he finally bows
he seems embarrassed to recall himself.
We too would forget ourselves,
clapping our hands like corpes
against this momentary wish to die.
In the silence when the final tremor of a string
has ceased — in that emptiness which holds everything
in its arms for an instant, tenderly, like an infant —
what is it but extinction that's longed for?

In the lobby at intermission
I see old friends I don't know well,
their eyes glazed as they drift by me
like shades in their solitary courses:
old Mrs. Harris, the dirt of the grave already on her face,
her gaze smiling but vacant,
scrubbed Jason in blazer and gold-striped tie,
his fourth-form mind secretive as arches
in a prep school of red brick,
a weary man himself tomorrow like banker Smith, perhaps,

whose Breughel-red martini jowls
have slackened from the sadness of the piece,
widowed now and gone before I know it
over morning coffee, tart marmalade and toast,
the obiturary I read a scanty substitute
for one last conversation, that closure
a tonic one always seems to count on.

Now flickering lights have called us back
but how can I hear music without sorrow,
the lives of small friends like unplayed chamber works
only half composed inside the head?
Cantabile, yes, but we are Schoenberg after all,
our notes random and serial,
predicatable though never quite to be repeated.

TO A YOUNG MUSEUM GUARD

In blue livery unfit for a king
she stands more or less
at attention,
her white gloves unsullied by art.

A pillar of late empire,
she holds the building up
like a caryatid grown clumsy
on the wage of her subsistence.

Watching her watch,
she knows that time is money,
that money is marble, giltwood
and paint.

If you look too long
she returns your stare,
afraid of what you might be thinking,
afraid of what she does not know.

She would love it if every day were Monday
and the stone rolled away from the tomb.

You wouldn't find her here
or anywhere that beauty needed memory
or colors for the world to pay for
time and time again.

On her day off she goes to the beach,
for a moment finds herself
like Venus freezing in the foam.

MONHEGAN REVISITED

Gull cry and love cry run with the wind
then hover where the wrecked hull sprawls
rusty and rudderless in July sunshine.
Now both are lost where the boat,
on its side and lonely, hove to long ago.
Old roses climb the fishhouse wall,
weathered and beaten brown;
they bob like buoys on the turn of tide,
pink and sweet as unsalted guts.

On summer's cliffs too sheer for us
we lay where lichen gilded the great stones
and juniper haunted crevices,
huge fissures where the body
wakened like a child
(later gin could not bridge them,
its medicine a clear dream
of the green places gone foggy).
The mailboat roiled — coming and going —
her wake a wash of queasy islands
leeward and out of reach.

Just out of reach like love
or the small bleached deer bone
ledge-bound and white as snow,
frail relic of summer remembering itself,
always remembering itself.

FLAGSTAD REMEMBERS

Because I sang for Hitler,
my art was no less pure.
My hands were no less white,
and my third act so sure
it shook the heavens.

I might have held my peace
and let some lesser singer grace the stage,
but why not let one higher note
surmount the shrillness of a tyrant's rage?

History has been written,
and now it seems I was too gross.
Perhaps.
And yet the truth could not have slept:
As my Isolde soared, the monster wept.

ELEGY FOR A WAR CRIMINAL

The sea was cold and you were not forgiven.
Angel of death, I pity the hunted
though once you were a hunter,
your radiant unearthly smile
anathema to downcast eyes
that every morning watched your hand,
sterile and white,
gesturing who might live, who die.

In Paraguay
they found a bed still warm
though you of course had fled,
dived deeper into shadows,
the past your only future,
absconded like a god without love
from the horror of creation,
though how to work the hardest trick of all,
the *ex nihilo* in reverse?
On your nightstand the steel-blue luger,
merciful, efficient,
consoled you with the promise
of eternal sleep,
but when the moment came,
who to aim it at,
the hunter or the hunted?
Toward the end
you were kinder and kinder to children
and small animals

though perpetually insomniac,
afraid of nightmares that shook your limbs
and, waking, of the deeper certainty that rest
would always be impossible.

The day of your death the sea was calm,
glacier-cold and smooth as glass,
but you kept swimming farther and farther out,
the small life left you ditched on shore
like a windswept beach ball, its blood-red hue
a hole in bone-white sand.

In the chaos of water you still craved light
for the cave of your chest
where the fragments of a mirror rattled
and rattled then sank without sunshine
under shark shadow or the groupers' lair.

With no stake in the heart to hold it,
your corpse would rise again.

BEATUS ILLE
Lieutenant Siegfried von Strode
Berlin, April 1941

My colonel, one leave, has gone to see his wife.
His plunder, ranking very high indeed,
can hardly fail to please:
A sketch by Titian of Christ's final sob,
a golden dagger with a ruby knob
said to be Napoleon's,
a Stradivarius which nobody can play.
They will go to Götterdämmerung with Hitler,
where doubtless all will weep.
For me, the things I loved do not remain intact,
though semblances survive.
This afternoon a *Magic Flute*,
then Sekt on the Kurfürstendamm.
A balanced music orchestrates my sleep —
the birdcatcher and his wife
in martial strains panting till you weep
with laughter —
but still I wake to Wagner.

I remember a tiny bookshop and the curious Jew
who sought for me the choicest, oldest Horace,
incurable and rare and bound in sheepskin
from a Sabine farm.
In Turkish slippers, with his violin
he picked out Bach partitas line by line,

his drooping head musical and mute.
No doubt of it; in spite of all his grumbling
he was thankful just to be alive.
Happy the man who lies in beechen shade,
happy the shade who lies beyond the reach of men.
One day they dragged him to a pen
of huddling Jews shivering in a trainyard.
When I went back, a hard blond woman
told me they had found his papers forged.
But the violin was good, she said,
tapping her fingers on painted wood,
the old Cremona red like a hemorrhage
in her hands.
I had to go on living,
though hardly for the glory of the Reich,
my duty like a cicatrice on a boy's raw face,
permanent, disfiguring.
Be glad you stroked the cheek's fresh fire once,
the slim cadet you cradled in your lap
unsabered in tunic and grey peaked cap.
This little photograph? It's yours,
the silver locket with emblazoned door
about to close forever.

The war drags on, a hideous fiction
narrated by an idiot Führer
and yet, to judge by our response,
an art informs at all.

I saw the young men of France on fire,
wriggling like strawmen in the lacerating wire.
The pages of apocalypse?
I tear them out of early books
routinely now,
the double-headed eagle of St. John
taloned and indifferent
as a god without love.

I had a dream last night.
How the furs on your coat came alive
and threatened to devour you.

How the car which took me to the Russian front
struck and killed a nightingale in flight.
Then a deafmute standing idly in the road
grinned and pointed to an autumn field.
A butterfly was clinging to an orange weed,
and the flames of his wings as he pulsed and expired
could not be told from the rank and gaudy flower
which he hung upon.

THE ESCAPE ARTIST

He is always under ice
breathing air in that miraculous small space
between the water and its crueller glass

or in a fishtank drowning on a stage
hands bound behind his back
the bubbles from his mouth desperate as prayers

though no words can save the writhing body
that much you tell yourself
as watching you waste the last of his oxygen.

But that is his genius: to seem to suffer
as he sees you sigh,
to find the freedom of his uncuffed hands
and then to leave you manacled
as if his skill had slighted all along
and you alone could not escape.

How easy for him, how hard for you
this spectacle of showmanship so sure
the agony seems endless

though what confounds you finally is the grin —
radiant, perverse, inscrutable —
inflated on the surface where you sink.

THE ICONOCLAST
(For N.J.H.)

Your carved madonna, beautifully broken,
smiles her cinquecento smile.
Invisible hands, snapped off at the wrist,
hold only air with invisible tenderness.
Too heavy for human arms, the child
was severed centuries ago:
he lies now where the truth lies,
beyond the saving vanities of art.

I can believe in nothing but this,
a virgin's ruddy lip
crumbling to powder,
her abundant empty lap
forsaken of flesh,
her face a smooth oblivion
of pain,

can trace the true cross anywhere
in a garden, a stone, a gathering,
in all forms worn away by time,
in darkness and in light,
in the veriest vacancy of air.

APRIL

Despondent now, the orange robin squats
in the patter-pitter of perverse rain.
But still the blood prevails; she beaks her knots
this Spring to weave a fragile nest again.

Aunt Sarah, childless and unwed, once swept
a broken bird with tears into the hedge.
Maiden and austere, when at last she wept
it was for feathered doom upon a ledge.

She saw the shattered thing, and then the glass
that shielded her. Beyond she saw her face,
and then the oblivion of green grass.
The hand that plucked at death was cuffed in lace.

Later, nothing was said about the tears
or of the curled and withered robin's legs,
although it hardly took an ear to hear,
in her belly, the crush of azure eggs.

ANNIE

That spring we lived from high to high.
Fresh flowers in the front room,
your lilac in milk glass,
and everywhere faint whisperings
of mauve.
Our landlocked luxuries —
shrimp sandwiches and icy gin —
defied an oceanic loneliness
while we in ambience of afternoon
loved like angels
in the thin, thin air.

Sad flower child of the sun,
one March you hit Ohio on the run
then disappeared without the slightest warning
in the scud and storm of April.
They found your car in Texas,
though you had long since taken wing,
seeking a sky of sacrifice, azure
and devoid of love, beyond the human,
and purer than rain or pain.
A lover died in Berkeley of the drug.

Once you wrote to say you'd seen the quetzal.
Now from the detritus of years I see,
as through the rank luxuriance of memory,
somewhere on the jungle floor,
o somewhere staring up at me
in savage Aztec sadness,
the broken clay fragment of a mask.

FOR HERACLITUS

The brook gives me sparkles plenty.
A.R. Ammons

Mostly specious though a few
with the glint of real diamonds
the old possibilities
so many rhinestones now
in a stream darkening
to the final purpose
of its current,
a pool without reflection
that finds in stillness
the depth of its perfection.

What has become of the quick
light water
you only stepped in once
the rill running by you
as if your unaltering foot
were immortal?

Strange
how in the long bend of flow
you never gained the other side
at all
but kept to the middle
as one does
with everything suddenly over your head

46

and the whole river closing above you
at last
and the ripples you made
not reaching the far shore.

Who knew the bottom of it?

OCTOBER

My little son comes home from school,
his tireless grin broad this afternoon
as he waves a fistful of colored leaves
the teacher told him to gather
at recess.
They are for his mother and me
he says, with pride,
then flings them on the kitchen table
carelessly,
his tiny fingers mangling
the red and yellow edges
as he loses interest in what's done for.
He seems to say by this
if we are pleased, fine,
but no longer are they of any worth to him.

In the afternoon golden as a pear
he storms on to television, Orange Crush,
and the need for new sneakers
(he knows he has to buy them for "gym"
but is puzzled because there's no boy by that name
in his class).
He would hate to fall out of a tree,
he announces over Devil Dogs,
then chatters of the licking Tommy got
(his parents divorced)
for throwing acorns down
on the passing cars below.

48

His mother has gone out of the house
to have some time to herself
and I am here waiting for her
and for winter
with the last shadow of leaf
perhaps already fallen
with a little flutter
between us.
In my lap the boy squirms
as great bent branches
encircle him.
I hold him as tight as I can
knowing he won't stay still.

TEACHING MY SON TO TALK

We go to the farm near nightfall
(hardly a farm at all now
hemmed in as it is by houses
of equal shape and color)
though the walls are white as a temple still
and the work of the old clapboards holds
and there's a red barn sagging
from the weight of generations
like a father's heart about to burst.

The game is name and point
as I show him the animals for the first time
and he repeats them syllable by syllable
with little thuds
in this paradise already fallen
like a ripe apple in the grass
its time come.
Peering into bovine eyes
that glow like wild honey
in the twilight
he says after me "cow,"
his awe so original he dares to touch
the enormous wet nose
though only for the briefest second,
his tiny arm recoiling
like a serpent after striking.

Soon it's "chicken," "duck," "goose,"

then "pig" and "pony,"
"rabbit," "rooster," and "lamb"
in a cacophony of names
pungent as a barnyard
until I want to say
"son, these are the things themselves
unsullied by syntax or desire,
love them beyond language
for their immanence
the incense of dung and milk commingling
in the holy shadows of late light
here in this cathedral of barn
where the animals in their eloquence
praise the great creator
with their silence."

But he is tired and nodding now
the litany on his tongue
mechanical and fading fast
as his lids grow heavy
and he no longer points.
He says "cow, nice cow
bye-bye pony
good goose good goosey
go sleep now
go sleep."

THE NIGHT BEFORE CHRISTMAS

He falls asleep
changing his will in his mind,
who to leave to, who not to,
though even dead drunk
he knows that he himself
is worthless.

Somewhere are distant nieces and nephews,
distant cousins,
their Christmas cards
on the mantel
a tinselled reminder
that Scrooge still has a chance.

All are dispensable as reruns
in a house without a wife;
Were they so great —
Alastair Sim's, or Jimmy Stewart's,
or somebody else's wonderful life?
Perhaps. But what earthly use
are jingle bells, helping hands, or wings?

In the end he decides
on the animal league,
remembers the green-black
and grey stripes
of an abandoned tabby,
the pitiless yellow eyes
that asked for nothing

as she circled and circled
the narrow cage.
The cool touch of her nose
through the bars
felt like a snowflake
on the booze-numb knuckles
of his fist.

He weeps — not because he loves —
(that is unimportant now),
but because what has been most
to him has been littlest and least.

EASTERN CEMETERY
PORTLAND, MAINE

You contemplate the names
and they die again in memory,
as if the death of earth
were a small death only,
a parody of eons
felt and then forgotten
here where lilac bursts
and then luxuriates
unloved by legions underground.

Caught in a crazy chemistry
of clouds and sea and sky,
a reciprocity of blue and cream
as in Boudin
where heaven mirrors water
they cannot know how space and time
are curved and everything returns
to states we have no names for.

Forgive me. I cannot give them up
but need them here to ask:
"What did you make of it,
this old diurnal course of roots and stars,
the purple crocus rigid in new snow?" —
though always they say "nothing,"
telling how time takes care of itself,

how the vireo comes back again
in a Springtime green without meaning
save for patterns we impose
cyclical and sad
like leaves flushing gold
and amber and then green again
(my pipe turned up this April
where I left it last October.
In the attic when the torrents came,
I scribbled verse against the dark).

We begin in love and end in love
and in between is poetry,
as with a house of cards
where all fall down at last.
And so their lives keep crying
to be lived again,
the old despairs and hungers,
failures and completions
undreamt of but real
like the perfect pear ruddy underfoot.
Let the new grass greening
stop my mouth
here where silence is a masterpiece,
the one sublime within my reach.

WALT WHITMAN, NIGHT NURSE

I.

In a shabby room in Camden with faded grass-green
    wallpaper
and printed roses that have lost their bold electric hue,
an old man watches out the window
for fresh male faces passing in the street,
for the stranger who waits there for him,
for eyes still fiery in their love of life.
Though his own sight is failing fast,
the wan white-bearded patriarch
misses almost nothing:
not the teamsters rowdy in liquor and brown leather,
two-days growth on raw-boned cheeks,
not the urchins, truant, who sass him with a wink
(they know a skinny-dipping stream a sharp delight
busy as birch brooms after school)
or the new grooms fresh as lilac
their bodies smooth as girls.
Not the soldiers, old and young,
whose hollow jaws must take him back
to the blue camps and hospitals of thirty years before,
to drum taps and the musky stench of war.

II.

A young unbearded man drifts like a shade among the
    beds —
row after row of them — where naked figures out of
    Dante
shudder in their pain, their hopeless wounds a hell
of fire licking like a nimbus at the flesh,
their only heaven now a dream of ether.
One man has lost a buttock, another a shoulder,
many have only semblances of faces
and those with maimed limbs only are thought lucky.
A drummer boy is blind and cannot see he has no feet.
Screams are ordinary, day and night,
as surgeons make their rapid, unpitying rounds.
Silence is rare, but not the breaking down
of males once strapping, sobbing now like boys,
their cries a scalpel's edge scraping the stillness.
Excrement, sweat and chloroform choke the air.
Bodies come and go in the moveable feast which is
    death.

The ones he stays with longest are the sickest,
striplings neither boys nor men,
the ones who haven't lived and never will,
sprawling like puppets on their death-white cots.
The offices he does — unspeakable —
he does with nameless tenderness,

cheerful and selfless as a mother.

His listens, tells stories, writes letters home
he knows will be the last
(refines the fevered phrases,
improves on fond farewells),
holds hands, dries eyes, smoothes brows,
closes with forefinger and thumb the sudden glaze
that makes him catch his breath and bow his head.
He knows that nothing is colder than a virgin's brow
or still red lips kissed for the last time.

Though some of the men think him odd,
none of the afflicted shun him.
He hovers like an angel by their beds,
his face an etching out of Blake
copper bright and clear as flame.

III.
In spite of all the pilgrims, writers, kindred spirits
(Wilde said the old man was himself a poem) —
he dies alone, his vigil at the window broken forever.
At dawn a troop of angels musters at the door,
the perfect bodies of the mangled men who died
come back to lead him to the promised land.
Voices are gruff but gentle, the way he liked,
their faces unearthly now like Leonardo's last
    St. John.

On a litter of gold they place the Sophoclean trash
that is an old man's body, lightly, so lightly,
then lead him though the air, their team of milk-white
     oxen docile as lambs.

By the river where they gather is a swimming hole like
     Jordon.
Youths plunge like Icarus from the trees,
their dolphin-crested strokes white wrigglings of delight.

All look on as angels strip the old man —
first the slouch hat, then the overalls and flannel shirt,
then the flesh itself until he has his perfect body back —
the smell of fresh-cut prairie grass rising from the
ground like incense.

Soon everyone is shouting, singing, clapping
for the new man who in the window of the stream
sees himself at last, electric, radiant,
neither boy nor man forever.

There is laughter in the shallows, splashing,
as the figure on shore weeps, his eyes hard as diamonds.
Then an adolescent voice, cracked but manly,
exhorts him from the rill:
"Jump Walt, jump."
And at last he does, arms outstretched like an eagle,
or a Phoenix being born.
No, like a swan who has sung her song.

NIGHTSCAPE WITH DOVES

New snow in the clearing.
Blank as a page,
the field remains unmarred,
obscure cuneiform of doves' feet
as yet unprinted,
though you hear a cry of birds,
clay-coloured mourners,
in a nearby margin of trees.
Because it is dusk
you cannot see their shapes
in the enveloping blackness.

The great night falls
and you are nearer wherever the end is,
but right now meaning is a sound
inexpressibly itself,
a trick much like the trick of happiness,
a completeness which knows
that the end of the book
is the last white page
you go on revising forever.